Invisible STRENGTH

A Book of Poetry

R. G. Ivey

ISBN 978-1-64191-439-0 (paperback)
ISBN 978-1-64191-440-6 (digital)

Christian Faith Publishing, Inc.
832 Park Avenue
Meadville, PA 16335
www.christianfaithpublishing.com

Printed in the United States of America

This is dedicated in remembrance of my late wife Gloria,
whom I will forever love. There is nothing greater than to know
Jesus, family, and friends. All abounding together
on one accord—love!

Contents

Preface

Come, let us together take a walk on a pathway that will lead us on an extraordinary poetic journey. It will open up a spiritual world of emotional expression, with a radiant light upon love, joy, faith, hope, grief, sorrow, strength, endurance, righteousness, loneliness, and solitude.

I was inspired to embark on the writing of poetry after the unexpected and sudden death of my wife Gloria. We enjoyed a happy marriage together for forty-seven years, after a prior four years of dating. She was always telling me that I should be a little more serious about writing and consider sharing my thoughts with others.

Gloria had a wonderful gift of encouragement and shedding light on those merit that lie deep within the soul. Writing was one of those hidden talent for me, which she would so eloquently bring to my attention. After writing "The Dove of My Life," a poem that I presented to Gloria on her seventieth birthday, she would say things like "Your words are so inspirational and would brighten the hearts of so many people."

A month before her birthday, I was touched by the Holy Spirit and had the urge to pen another poem. I then wrote the poem "Comfort," which I later shared with her. This being seven months before her death, I didn't have any idea that I was describing the emptiness and loneliness of such a dark time that would be taking place in my own life.

The words that she had spoken earlier to me continued to resonate in my heart after her death in January 2017. Now I bring and share with you this wonderful gift of poetry, which was given to me and inspired by the Holy Spirit.

A Mist

As a mist we say about our life, how true it is to be
Fifty-one years ago you came along to share this life with me.
Through this walk that we are making together many challenges
     have appeared.
But now we understand that others may stand near.
The trials we faced from day to day have made us strong along our way.
We moved with passion, one step at a time, the dreams that we had
     was highly prime,
Our journey in life which we begin was one of faith and need
We did not understand the power of God indeed.
His love and grace has moved us along at such an important pace.
It's evident to say that He is the only way.
The little things that we overlook and fail to stop and see
Maybe the most important of all to help in our troubles when we
     begin to fall.
The quickness of life that passes us by is hard to comprehend.
Look back from time to time and see where you have been.

The Dove of My Life

So many years ago magic happened in my life when a beautiful
    dove appeared.
How majestic a statue of this goddess that God brought so near.
The pure radiance of her eyes and the gleaming of her taste,
Made her whole being smile as we met face to face.
I tried to greet her with a joyful sound,
But the words were muted as they abound.
Her hair was like silk as she turned about,
Which caused it to flow like waves of the ocean, free, and without
    doubt.
I entreated her with the snack of the day,
Popcorn was on the list for that I could only pay.
It brought a smile to her face and trembling to my knees,
As we shared this snack together she gave me a feeling of ease.
The thought of such a goddess to enter into my world,
Fulfilled the realities of life for me, which only God's mysteries reveal.
The dove that appeared for me from a region so afar
Is the shining star in my life that will always illuminate my heart.
Happy birthday to my beloved,
As Shulammite was to Solomon, so are you to me.

The Walk

Be not disillusioned by the mirror glow,
It is only a reflection of the outside you know.
The light that illuminates your heart and soul
Is of greater concern for it's the true control.
So let your steps be directed by the invisible God,
Who sees from within, and He started it all.
His views are of love, kindness, and grace,
Which surround us daily in an infinite way.
Your ways are higher, oh Lord,
And your thoughts are too,
We will understand them better when we are with you.
So let His light so shine in our hearts every day,
And guide our steps as we walk while He carries us on our way.

Music

The trees danced about for I know not where its music comes
Providing a feeling of peace while enjoying the dazzling charm.
A covering of gray in the middle of the day,
Has been pulled over the skies, giving off a dusk of dawn as it
prepares to have its way.
Creatures frolic around in flight and on the ground
Seeming not to care about the things that will abound.
The breath of music which caused the trees to dance
Give my soul a refreshing appeal as it sings around me still.
Liquid drops begin to fall, the thunder roars in my ears
Creatures no longer frolic about and seem to disappear.
An invisible God which I cannot see but feel all through the day
Has given me faith to understand the music that comes my way.

Comfort

Come, Holy Spirit, and heal my pain for I know not what to do.
You have always been a shelter for me when it begins to rain.
There is a deep emptiness, and my heart is severely torn.
The darkest of days is upon me, and I need the Savior's hand.
Come, Holy Spirit, and heal my pain for I know not what to do.
You have always been a shelter for me when it begins to rain.
The flower that always blooms for me with the renewing of every day
Has gone away from this life, now sprouts in a heavenly way.
There is no victory, there is no sting, which death once held for me,
    you see
The Savior's hand did come in a place called Calvary.
He took my stripes, and bore my sin, and died upon a cross.
He then went away and got the keys and set the captives free.
He sent me a comforter, for days such as this, to help me in my distress
While he prepares the rest.
Come, Holy Spirit, and heal my pain for you know what to do
And I will be still and give it all to you.

Invitation

In every way walk silently and listen as you go
The words that you hear may surprise you of the things you do not
    know.
Let your Spirit be energized and move you along with grace,
His unmerited favor brighten your heart and give you a better pace.
Take the limits off the Lord, let them disappear,
The cross that lies before you, pick it up and do not fear.
Completeness of your destiny is filled with love and joy
It's positioned with the Lord, that no one can destroy.
So open up your heart, be not afraid to invite Him in!
You will be amazed, let your new life begin.
Your mind will be renewed, each and every day.
The journey will get smoother as you tarry along your way.
Leaving behind old memories that once led you astray
No longer hold you in bondage for this is a brand new day.

Prayer

Beauty of this life that surrounds us with the dawning of each day
Should remind us daily of how important it is to pray.
The wonderful art in the heaven which is so majestically shown
Renders to our spirit that we are not alone.
Flickering of the stars at night blanketed by a sumptuous moon
Gives off a deep affection of love that we should all consume.
It intensifies the feeling of tenderness and warmth
With the interment attachment and solicitude in our thoughts.
There is only one so loving and caring in every way
The eternal God who brighten our world and bring pleasure
        without pay.
We owe it to the Lord
To praise Him as we may
Give Him all the glory,
And this is why we should pray.

Struggles

Life road seems long and difficult with struggles at every turn
The experience you gain that must be earned will later inspire your
    way
War takes place in your mind with principalities every day
The battle has already been won, victory is yours to stay
There is no condemnation for you so love and trust Jesus as Lord
Worldly fears and challenges that are within will constantly appear
    again
Be strong and courageous in your fight for the battle is the Lord's
The giants in your life will become small when you trust in His
    Holy Word
Precious blood of Christ was shed for you to take away all sin
So be of good cheer and do not fear, let His peace comfort your soul
The Holy Spirit will light your path as He did in days of old
To lead you through the struggles of time and bring boldness to
    your soul.

Emotional Waves

The waves of emotions that I feel from day to day
Is very difficult for me along this uncertain way.
It is unexplainable to the human ear
But the Lord has told me that I should not fear.
Challenges that we have is not always of ease,
But thank God for grace which will always please.
Walk with your head held high and let your countenance be one
    with a smile,
Your heart will respond in the greatest of trials.
A loving God who stands above all the waves
Will not let you go in the darkest of days.
He is always a present help as we move about
To protect us in our troubles and remove all doubt.
So trust and believe that your path will be made straight
Your Father God will be there, patient as He wait.

Branches

This is a moment that I cannot think, my mind is just a blur
Words are tangled that I want to speak, but I know not anymore.
It is time to step back from my own thoughts for now,
And let the Holy Spirit who guides show me just how.
He leads me where ever I go, directing on my path
The daily help that I truly need so his fruit will appear at last.
The wisdom that He gives to me from deep down in my soul
Is from the precious Vine that only God control.
Branches are meant to be just what they really are
Depending on the Vine of Life so they can flourish much more.
Pruning will take place at times as we move on
The abundance of fruit that is later revealed
Will teach us all how we should live.

Reminiscence of Time

Existence seems to get better with the passing of every day,
But the emptiness in my heart appears never to go away.
The mere thought of my beloved which is always near
As I reminisce about the past, it always brings a tear.
She was the dove of my life that flies with me each day,
And lands on my shoulder to help me along the way.
Life is so hard without her, my world has completely changed
Movement of a precious day take root in a different way.
So I take a stroll with God on the mountain top of my mind
My beloved is always present and with me all the time.
The comfort that He brings for my grief and distress,
Can only be explained by Him who strengthens and gives rest.
His peace is unknown to me, no question will I ask,
It is one of those great mysteries that only God possesses.

Blessing

When you live your life God's way, a brighter light will appear.
It gets easier, yet challenging, on a new road that will come near.
The world offers us many direction that we could take,
But destruction is at the end
So try the narrow gate, where you have never been
The blessing that awaits will be a surprise to you,
But they have always been there, waiting to bring you through.
Take a ride without your pride, don't let it get in your way.
The wrong turns that you've made will only lead you astray.
Leave the condemnation behind, the journey brought valuable gifts
Receive them with all your heart,
Your faith will hold fast and not let you drift.
The lamp is always at your feet that will give light as you go
There are many more blessing awaiting you
More than you'll ever know.

Light and Darkness

Darkness can bring one to the end of themself
With emptiness and void in tow
Making life feel meaningless,
For all of those who go.
Comprehending not, the true light that is within
Will overtake the darkness so that we can see again
Your plans for independence, being wholesome as they may
Can cause a vacuum in your space which may not be God's way.
He invested a lot because of His love when His son went to the cross,
A debt we made, but Jesus paid, to redeem us for we were lost.
There is a beautiful light which shines for all to see,
It began with creation, and darkness cannot retreat.
Submit yourself totally to Christ, do it without delay,
He has paid the ultimate price for you,
Yes! He is the only way.

Alone

Bring me home, oh Lord, I pray to thee,
It is so hard for me down here.
My love one has gone home and left me all alone.
Not so, my Lord responded,
I am always with you to stay.
Your loved one is here with me and very happy, I say.
There is work to be completed which you cannot see
When my plan for your life is done,
I'll bring you home with me.
You say that you're my servant, that trust is in your hands,
Be courageous in your faith, let me make all the plans.
I will be with you always, this promise will I make,
Forsaking thee is not my way, and Jesus stands at the gate.
I Am who I Am, filled with agape love,
Remember my word both day and night,
And you will make it through this treacherous fight.

Empty Presence

This house seems so large now, it never did before
Brightness of your spirit filled our home with love and more.
Deeply missed must I mention, your spirit is with me each day
As I look in your closet, precious thoughts come my way.
I speak as if you are here with me, conversation is not at loss.
Your presence covers every corner and room,
Which takes away the sadness and gloom.
We became as one in our life,
Our thoughts were always the same.
You read my feeling as a book,
That caused me to give a surprising look.
A marriage which was made in heaven, this would I always say.
Because the Lord played such a part,
We honored our vows from the very start.
Meaning not, this was a perfect case, the enemy always stood near
Waiting for an opportune time,
To steal our joy that his spirits may appear.
The struggles were always challenging,
It all worked out in the end.
Victory belonged to the Lord,
For He knew where we had been.

Protection

Dressed in God's armor from head to toe
Give us full security against the evil foe.
His territory is large,
That he travels with ease,
To caused turmoil in life and never to please.
His deeds are distrustful, we cannot fight him alone
Remember we have an advocate who sits on the throne.
Discernment of God's word, this we should all know
Understanding His truth and ways, giving Him our burden to tow.
The grace of God is protection that serves as a shield
It covers the saints completely for this is God's will.

Help in Distress

Moving on toward future days comes with resistance to do
Living a life without my spouse is a reality I must pursue.
Negative thoughts come into mind of things if I only had done
May have saved her precious life, and I would still have her
    wonderful charm.
Being in this existing fog, engulfed by a vaporous cloud
Dreams that we once had no longer speaks aloud.
Though important at the time carries no interest anymore.
Her absence, being part of me, brings despair right to my door.
These declining moods that rise and fall, materializing in every
    thoughts
Brings all pleasure which has been gained to a slow and painful halt.
Realizing this is the enemy with his destruction at full force
Causes me to cry out to God, for He is my powerful source.
Embracing me with His unconditional love, understanding the
    extent of pain
Sustains my physical suffering and bears this deceptive strain.

Resurrection and Grief

A time will come for all of us,
When this body we have returns to dust.
All of God's saints who do believe
Is given the Lord's guaranteed reprieve.
It is difficult emotionally when our loved ones depart
But eternal life is promised as they begin a new start.
Enjoy this day that you are given, don't overload your mind.
Hurting and wounds will all heal in the Lord's specific time.
The soul lives on, held in the Father's hands
Awaiting an immortal body, as the Lord has planned.
Filled with mercy and love, which He equally brings
A compassionate, sovereign God, creator of everything.
His glorious power of resurrection that all the world will see.
Shall secure an eternal future, both for you and me.

Nature Pleasures

Evidence of your love, oh Lord, is with me every day.
You speak with me ever so softly as I stroll along and pray.
The miracles of life surround us, open up your eyes and see.
Phenomenal features of nature with its amusing pleasures of glee.
Standing on the shore of the sea in the brilliance given by the sun.
Watching great waters before me with fascination, enchantment,
and charm.
Fishermen cast their lines in hope for the catch of the day
While beachgoers relax on sands and watch their families play.
With all the pleasures that we enjoy, how can anyone forget God's
grace?
Remember Jesus bore our sins and redeemed us from the enemy's
chase.
Receive this gift of righteousness, for you are heirs in the family of
God.
Be delighted with the grace He gives, we are all His children from
the very start.

Precious Words

Her spirit entered my soul as it did in days of old
Providing needed peace within, and many words left untold.
Removing her precious name from possession that we have gained
Brings sadness to my heart, but her spirit eased the pain.
These things must take place for this is the earthly law
To pursue your destiny in life, let go of this very small straw.
She spoke of things more meaningful and shared her love once more.
Encouraging words of comfort and peace, hold on to God's
    righteousness, never let go.
Pass on your spiritual qualities to improve family's needs and pray.
Leave them this legacy, none of us were meant to stay.
Holy Spirit is with you constantly, don't think you are traveling alone.
Let all you fears be diminished, the comforter is in your zone.
The beauty of heaven that awaits is unimaginable to you just now.
Enjoy God's goodness in the earth,
We will all meet again in this wonderful place.

Change

Gloomy days are upon me, where do I go from here?
The realities of life is threatened, a lonely change has come near.
To continue this journey alone, this thought never occurred to be.
Responsible powers for precious existence is taken for granted, you see.
Respect the recurrences of daily life, be reverent to the Lord each day
No promises are made for delay, we know not the length of our stay.
God will take the grayest of time, while adding a bow of light.
Showing a gesture of goodness and love, there isn't need to feel
    vulnerable or fright.
Personal strength will be depleted, power come from the Master's
    source.
God's love speaks with perfection, in His deliverance there is no
    discourse.
He is an asset in our weakness, lifting high above the abyss
Rely totally on Jesus Christ, you will be greeted with a pleasant kiss.

Encouragement

Embrace your Garden of Eden
Walk with God in the cool of the day.
If you have accepted Jesus Christ
As your Lord, His grace is here to stay.
Let the fruit trees grow and the flowers bloom, don't hinder in any way
The Lord is always standing by to carry you through your day.
Dress, tilt, and keep the earth the best that you know how
Don't worry about the stressful weeds for He will use His plow.
Embrace your Garden of Eden, be strong and do not stray,
Jesus Christ is your Savior and Lord, let Him lead the way.

Sweet Aroma

Sweet scent of the Holy Spirit refreshes the purity of air
This satisfying aroma of life brings full measure with all care.
Breathe in all this goodness, let it brighten while replenishing your soul
Feel the peace and joy of our Lord, His pure fragrances are untold.
Powerful is the aroma within can never alone be quenched
Enlighten my being completely and contaminate every inch.
Take not away this pleasant odor, it is perfume to my heart
Knowing that Jesus abide in me to fill the emptiness and never part.
Enjoy the redolence of this spiritual bouquet, it's the freshest you'll
      ever know,
Jesus Christ made it possible, He is the ointment that heals as we go.
Take a whiff of this wonderful fragrance, let your nose lead you His
      way.
The smell of eternal glory will fulfill your hunger each day.

Choices

My sight will remain fixed upon the Lord, He will direct and lead
for me
Jesus is the true guide of life although we have eyes to see.
His vision is much more superior, nothing escapes His view
The creator of all things and loving, which include me and you.
Freely giving a gift of grace and righteousness, to accept it or not is
your choice
Available to all who receive Him, for he died to give us a voice.
The decision made is eternal, use wisdom when you choose.
Put your faith in the Lord, you will never feel faint or lose.
With great power He stands before us, bridging a chasm impossible
to cross
By accepting Jesus as your Lord, unmerited favor is gained, absent
the cost.
Supreme ruler of time and space, absolute sovereignty is His alone.
His love for us is unwavering, praise God, the Lord is on the
throne.

The Plan

In your honor, oh Lord, I suffer for your name
Being a living sacrifice this light shines for your fame.
To understand your plan, sometimes is hard to view
It was also hard for Jesus, when He bore the cup from you.
Jesus's redeeming blood bought life for us in the presence of our sin
Reconciling us back with the Father and giving a clear slate again.
Your will must be done in this life to fulfill your glorious plan
Our minds are too finite for the picture you have at hand.
Faith and trust in you, oh God, is all we need for now.
Manifestation of things unseen will appear, but we don't know how.
To be your vessel every day can bring difficult task for sure
But I stand ready to meet the challenge that I may bring glory to you.
The light of your glory waits, illuminating heaven and earth
An unseen wonder in your plan brighten the beauty of new birth.

Praise

The Lord has taken me out of debt and freed me from all sin
Placing it all on His shoulders, justifying us from the bondage we
    were in.
I will praise you in the earth, as I will above in heaven
The redeeming blood of Jesus has saved me now and forever.
What a wonderful gift to freely give to such a sinful man
Being that the Lord is the only way, Jesus took this mighty stand.
He set me apart for His service, this is an honor for me to own
For He is worthy and should be praised, all the glory is His alone.
My faith and trust will always be to a gracious God who set me free
His love is easy for me to see, just look at the blood He shed on the
    tree.
Don't take this view so lightly, it is not a mythical thought.
Jesus is alive, in the believers a redeemed life has been bought.

Options

Many options in life are given, what choices shall I make?
Destruction stands along the road, contingent on the path you take.
Although bondage has been lifted, the spirit of the enemy is alive
Be vigilant in your reasoning, he will introduce selfish pride.
Considering the facts at hand, wisdom is here if we seek.
Let her help in these decision and empty yourself as she speaks.
By gaining knowledge through her, assurance on this journey is
    guaranteed.
Difficult challenges which are faced daily will get easier as you are
    freed.
Be not afraid to follow, a prosperous travel this will be
The picture of life will encompass you, it is all waiting for us to see.
Joy is yours for the taking, happiness is the choice you make
Be wise in your decision, you will enter through a wonderful gate.

Image

True guidance for our direction, dear Lord, is only found in and
    through you.
Your life was given for us to see, the amazing love that will forever be.
In your image, oh God, you created me, true love consistently
    shines through.
Even in my disobedience and sin, grace abound much more from you.
The carnal nature that I behold is in this body which sin controlled
A worldly system filled with lust, my belief in the Lord I put my trust.
He trains me daily to make me strong, the obstacles before me are hard
A crown that I will later receive was all His coaching from the start.
It will be a pleasure to be more like Him, a personal friend the Lord
    will be
To be conformed to His likeness, by the Holy Spirit He put in me.
Work and train with endurance every day, it is all for the Lord in
    the end
He has wiped away all your guilt and sin,
So don't be concerned with where you have been.

No Ending

When our life began, we did not have a say
But later found out that the Lord would lead the way.
Unwise choices have been made, many led us astray
Following a worldly path in life, never thinking to stop and pray.
Costly decision was ours alone, your eyes weren't open to see
The problems that were caused, none of them had to be.
Praying to God and asking, how can this situation go away?
It was at that time realized, all we have to do is pray.
Begin by asking the Lord to come into your life.
By accepting Him as Savior, no longer will you pay the price.
My eyes was then opened, and now I could clearly see
The importance of walking with God,
By reading His word daily, it would carry me.
There was no choice to be made, in the beginning of your life.
There is no ending either, for eternal life is in Christ.

Embrace the Now

Remembering my history not so long ago, many things of a
    wonderful past
The happiness and joy we experienced, I thought would forever last.
The hole in my heart is wide and deep, seems as though nothing
    can compare
It is a different experience for all of us, but we should never give up
    in despair.
Another day has glistened for me to see, yesterday moved into the past
No thought should be given of tomorrow, explore today's
    wonderment, indulge in its task.
I looked toward the heavens, the formation of clouds was prone,
A celestial figure appeared above me, moving gracefully across the
    endless dome.
It enlighten my heart with wonder, how the Lord is with me each day
This journey is about His glory, Holy Spirit will paved the way.
These moments should be cherished with fullness throughout the day
Perfect is God's plan for our life, embrace it with joy, ceasing not to
    pray.

Candles

Aroma of the incense is fading, but I know that the scent will return
It is always present at solitary moments, reminding me often of
    greater concerns.
Daily life progresses onward, where it is going I do not know
I must take this ride along, for it will lead me where I should go.
The aroma appears frequently, especially when things are off course
Bringing me back to reality that I may focus on the genuine source.
I remember the smell extremely well, from when you were here
    with me
The candles that you burned so often, how lovely the fragrance
    would be.
My travels are never solely alone, the wonders of the Lord are great
To fill my heart with your presence is truly a mystery I will take.
Therefore I count it all as a blessing, remembering what God
    promised before
He is always present in me, to heal the lonely heart and more.

About the Author

A lover of God and a follower of Jesus Christ as a disciple, I have personally and continue to experience the power of the Holy Spirit in my daily life, and bear witness to His amazing love that He has for us all.

I am a Viet Nam veteran that received several medals in war to include the Purple Heart, a retired Law Enforcement Officer and a Graduate of Roger Williams University.

My service toward fulfilling the great commission given to us by our Lord and Savior Jesus Christ has varied in many capacities, to mention a few, as a teacher, mentor, counselor and prison ministry.

I continue to strive forward to touch the lives of others and bring them into a saving relationship by faith in our Lord and Savior Jesus Christ. There is much work to be done, and I am graceful to be a vessel for the Lord.

A family that deeply and truly love the Lord, I am the well pleased father of a wonderful daughter, son, and daughter-in law, and grandfather to four delightful grandchildren,

This book of poetry that I bring to you will serve as a beacon of hope toward many challenges that are faced now and later in a dying world, while encouraging believers not to become a victim of condemnation from pasted events.